Chief of Space Operations' Planning Guidance

1st Chief of Space Operations

CSO Priorities

- *Empower a Lean and Agile Service*

- *Develop Joint Warfighters in World Class Teams*

- *Deliver New Capabilities at Operationally Relevant Speeds*

- *Expand Cooperation to Enhance Prosperity and Security*

- *Create a Digital Service to Accelerate Innovation*

"We are forging a warfighting Service that is always above. Our purpose is to promote security, assure allies and partners, and deter aggressors by demonstrating the capability to deny their objectives and impose costs upon them. We will ensure American leadership in an ongoing revolution of operations in space, and we will be leaders within government to achieve greater speed in decision-making and action. We will partner with and lead others to further responsible actions in, and use of, space to promote security and enhance prosperity. Should an aggressor threaten our interests, America's space professionals stand ready to fight and win."

General John W. Raymond

INTENT

This Chief of Space Operations' Planning Guidance (CPG) provides foundational direction for the Space Force to advance National and Department of Defense (DoD) strategic objectives. This authoritative Service-level planning guidance supersedes previous guidance and provides the context and outline for our new Service design. In some areas, the CPG will define specific actions, timelines and offices of primary responsibility. In other areas, the CPG describes my intent and desired outcomes. This guidance is intended to empower space professionals at all echelons to take initiative consistent with their delegated authority and mission focus to implement Service priorities. To enable initiatives, I will also specify several efforts that should be deprioritized to generate resources for reinvestment.

This CPG communicates my intent and defines the capabilities and culture the USSF will pursue over my tenure. I will update intent, expand on guidance and review the progress of transformation initiatives via Force Design guidance annually. I expect all echelons to read, understand and implement this guidance.

The Space Force has a mandate in national strategy, policy, and law to be both pathfinder and protector of America's interests as a space-faring nation. The convergence of proliferating technology and competitive interests has forever re-defined space from a benign domain to one in which we anticipate all aspects of human endeavor – including warfare. The return of peer, great power competitors has dramatically changed the global security environment and space is central to that change.

The United States Space Force is called to organize, train, equip, and present forces capable of *preserving America's freedom of action in space; enabling Joint Force lethality and effectiveness;* **and** *providing independent options – in, from, and to space.* Demonstrable and persistent military spacepower promotes security in the space domain and assures partners. Spacepower backstops deterrence by communicating America's ability to impose costs on hostile actors and deny adversary objectives. Security and stability set conditions for a range of national and partner interests in all domains and enhance America's long-term competitive advantage and leadership.

While the Industrial Age created our nation's early advantage in space, the tools and skillsets of the Information Age are required to sustain and extend that advantage. The rapidly increasing scale, scope, complexity, and pace of space domain operations in general, and military space operations in particular, demand an independent space Service. The change in policy and law that created the Space Force followed closely on the heels of the 2017 National Security Strategy and 2018 National Defense Strategy, and their bold, future focus informs our force design. We will deliver a streamlined, agile, and innovative organization that sets a new standard in the Department of Defense.

During this period of transformation, our forces must continue to deliver the effects our Nation and Joint Force count on without fail. Commanders responsible for those missions will prioritize efforts to ensure they continue seamlessly despite the disruptions inevitable during Service establishment. This CPG outlines my priorities to guide how the Space Force will organize, train, equip, integrate, and innovate:

> *Empower a Lean and Agile Service*
> *Develop Joint Warfighters in World Class Teams*
> *Deliver New Capabilities at Operationally Relevant Speeds*
> *Expand Cooperation to Enhance Prosperity and Security*
> *Create a Digital Service to Accelerate Innovation*

These priorities will guide Service efforts across all echelons, shape performance assessment at Headquarters U.S. Space Force, and frame how we communicate to civilian leaders across and outside the DoD. They provide a strong foundation for where we want to be as a Service over the next decade, beyond the tenure of any one CSO, Administration, or Congress.

Space Force will offer civilian leaders and Joint Commanders options that can be used independently or in combination to deter or defeat aggression and achieve national objectives. While we will extend and defend America's competitive advantage in peacetime, **the ultimate measure of our readiness is the ability to prevail should war initiate in, or extend to space.**

America's Space Force will be *Semper Supra*, always above. We are moving swiftly to establish a lean, agile, and innovative Service ready to meet the challenges of today and the future. We stand ready to protect and deter, and to fight and win in freedom's high frontier.

STRATEGIC CONTEXT

DESIGN IMPERATIVE

America needs a Space Force able to deter conflict, and if deterrence fails, prevail should war initiate in or extend to space. Space capabilities enhance the potency of all other military forces. Our National leadership requires resilient and assured military space capabilities for sustained advantage in peaceful competition, or decisive advantage in conflict or war.

We will design and build a Space Force to meet three cornerstone responsibilities: preserve freedom of action, enable Joint lethality and effectiveness, and provide independent options – in, from, and to space. We must build a force that allows civilian decision makers and Joint commanders to fully exploit the space domain to achieve National strategic objectives.

The change in the geo-strategic and operating environment that compelled the creation of the Space Force means that many of our legacy space capabilities must be reevaluated for ongoing relevance. **Let me be clear – if we do not adapt to outpace aggressive competitors, we will likely lose our peacetime and warfighting advantage in space.**

The process of designing and building a new Service requires productive disruption. We cannot deliver the new capabilities the Nation requires while remaining indistinguishable from the ways and means of our past. **I expect commanders and program managers to accept moderate risk associated with innovation and experimentation to build an agile force that better ensures our long-term competitive advantage in space.**

Failing to accept the risk that accompanies innovation and experimentation will slow capability development and ultimately transfer risk to Joint warfighters. I do not accept the imposition of risk on warfighters to protect bureaucratic processes.

We face twin challenges: we will not be bold enough, or that risk-aversion and legacy-oriented processes will undermine our efforts. The first challenge is my charge to all space professionals – be bold, your leaders and your Nation expect it. The second is the responsibility of Service senior leaders – lead boldly and inspire bold leaders inside and outside the Service.

RISE OF COMPETITVE GREAT POWERS

Chinese and Russian military doctrines indicate they view space as essential to modern warfare, and view counterspace capabilities as potent means to reduce U.S. and allied military effectiveness. Modern Chinese and Russian space surveillance networks are capable of finding, tracking, and characterizing satellites in all earth orbits. Both Russia and China are developing systems using the electro-magnetic spectrum, cyberspace, directed energy, on-orbit capabilities, and ground-based antisatellite missiles to destroy space-based assets. These systems can achieve a range of effects against U.S. and allied military, civil and commercial capabilities from temporary and reversible, to irreversible degradation.

In addition to holding our own space capabilities at risk, systems fielded by peer competitors increasingly allow them to operate with the reach, agility, and lethality that U.S. forces once unilaterally enjoyed. Both China and Russia continue to improve their space-based intelligence, surveillance, and reconnaissance (ISR) and communications capabilities to support long-range kill-chains that hold U.S. and allied terrestrial forces at risk.

In addition to space capabilities, **both China and Russia have elevated information superiority and decision speed to be central tenants of their doctrine.** The ability to observe, orient, decide, and direct action at machine speeds will revolutionize future military operations. This is especially true in space where spacecraft operate at speeds and distances orders of magnitude greater than terrestrial counterparts. The force that prepares for this revolution and reaps its potential will have a significant advantage over the force that does not.

PROLIFERATING ACCESS TO SPACE

The rapid growth of the commercial space sector provides the United States both new potential partners and opportunities to leverage commercial investment to enhance our space capabilities. Ubiquitous technology reduces barriers to access space for all and introduces new actors, competitors, and potential adversaries. Advantage will go to those who not only create the best technologies, but who also best integrate, field, protect, and operate them in ways that provide significant military advantages.

MISSION EVOLUTION: PAST, PRESENT AND FUTURE

When the space age began, mastery of the most advanced disciplines of science, engineering, and manufacturing was required to produce *a few exquisite systems*. Early military space systems were designed for strategic missions such as detecting ballistic missile launches. In the 1960s, the Soviet Union actively developed anti-satellite (ASAT) capabilities to attack the small inventory of U.S. military satellites. From that time on, the mission of space professionals had changed to include *defense of exquisite military space systems*.

New technology and the innovation of our operators and industry pressed these limited number of high value strategic space systems into unforeseen operational and tactical applications. The 1991 Gulf War was the first "space war" to fully integrate America's space capabilities on the battlefield. The dominant advantage that space-based ISR, satellite-based communication (SATCOM) and the Global Positioning System (GPS) gave Coalition forces led potential adversaries to consider space systems attractive targets in future conflict. Recent resurgence in deployment of modern direct assent and co-orbital ASAT capabilities require us to develop and deliver offensive and defensive options in the near-term, while we transition to a *resilient architecture able to mitigate attack, assure capabilities, and rapidly reconstitute* in the mid- to long-term.

Every interaction in space, between military, government, civil, and commercial entities creates a pattern of behavior that communicates intent and establishes, reinforces, or diminishes norms. Our space domain awareness capabilities allow us to compare intent as communicated by words and behaviors. Alignment between what an actor claims to be doing and what we observe, such as who initiates movement to proximity with another spacecraft, or who does – or does not – respond to requests to maneuver responsibly, refines our understanding of an actor's intent. *We will actively use interactions, consistent with applicable law, to shape norms of behavior that enhance National security and reduce opportunity for a competitor or potential adversary to misinterpret intent.*

Aware of substantial U.S. military strength on the land, in and under the sea, and in the air, potential adversaries are using asymmetric counters to mitigate U.S. power projection. Great power adversaries have used aggression and illegal occupation to seize territory, and

invested heavily in "anti-access and area-denial" (A2/AD) capabilities to make the air, sea, and land of their near-abroad inaccessible to an American or Coalition intervention. Space capabilities expose the vertical flank of the terrestrial A2/AD environment. **In the future multiple missions currently conducted by terrestrial forces will shift, in whole or in part, to space.** This is already underway with tactical ISR and will soon expand to other missions.

⟁ Empower a Lean and Agile Service

REDUCING BUREAUCRACY

The new design of our Space Force headquarters and Field Command structure aligns complementary functions and streamlines echelons of command in the deliberate pursuit of speed and agility. Space Force will innovate and incubate faster, flatter decision and command structures that can be refined and applied across the Department of Defense.

During the analysis that led to the creation of the Space Force, Congress identified over 60 offices responsible for elements of space policy, oversight, and guidance, with nearly 30 more who influence space architecture. We will work across the Department to unify and harmonize efforts. We will prepare implementation plans to unify disparate acquisition and sustainment authorities for space systems currently distributed across the Army, Navy, and Office of the Secretary of Defense.

The imperative to flatten bureaucracy is about more than efficient management – it enables the decision-making speed and agile implementation that generate advantage in competition or conflict. Our current system struggles to keep pace with fast evolving threats and technologies. Today's modernization efforts must navigate a slow, disaggregated and desynchronized bureaucratic process that increases risk for our Joint warfighters. We will consolidate and coordinate disparate processes to accelerate decisions and reduce that risk.

Reducing bureaucracy does not mean eliminating the oversight required by law and policy. Rather, it emphasizes empowerment through delegation of decision authority to the most responsive competent authority, and a high degree of accountability. **Tight alignment of responsibility, accountability, and authority is key to speed and agility.**

HEADQUARTERS U.S. SPACE FORCE DESIGN

Our smaller, more empowered force will be reflected in a smaller, more streamlined headquarters structure, re-formatted to merge direction of aligned functions under four new offices.

The Human Capital Office (HCO) will build and manage our workforce of the future. They will develop a human capital strategy that emphasizes up-to-date and innovative approaches to access, engage, assess, and retain world class civilian and military professionals. Their primary responsibility is to win the battle for talent, now and in the future. They will tailor force development to produce expertly trained and effectively led space professionals with the skills and mindset to sustain U.S. advantage in competition and prevail in war against a peer adversary. They will capitalize on our small Service size to enable talent management practices that individually develop, retain, manage, and cultivate high impact professionals.

The Operations Office will enable our space operations and training commands. They will oversee unit and capability readiness and develop force presentation options for the Secretary of the Air Force. They will integrate intelligence and operational policy to outpace threats and sustain a high-end ready spacecrew program; direct integrated analysis to assess performance of Space Force systems, personnel, and processes; and ensure the CSO can manage the readiness of forces. In addition, they will develop and represent USSF positions as Service operations deputy in support of the CSO as a Joint Chief. Under the Operations Office, the USSF Senior Intelligence Officer will build a space ISR enterprise to support operations, inform Service design and development, and enhance civilian and military decisions.

The Strategy and Resources Office (SRO) will drive USSF strategy, planning, and programming to ensure our force is resourced to succeed. They will lead USSF capability development, serve as resource champion for space capabilities, and influence the design of the national space architecture. The SRO will lead coordination with Combatant Commands to ensure the USSF POM position optimizes Joint effectiveness and lead partner engagement to ensure complementary allied, commercial and civil capability development.

In order to accelerate our Service transformation to a data-driven "digital service," we have created a new Technology and Innovation Office (TIO). The TIO will direct USSF innovation and incorporation of advanced technology. In addition, the TIO will work with the HCO to drive the technical culture and competencies of our Space professionals. The TIO will ensure the USSF has the data infrastructure and machine augmentation to embrace cutting edge information age organizational practice.

The USSF Director of Staff will generate a comprehensive, yet succinct hierarchy of business rules and directives that define roles and responsibilities within the headquarters enterprise. They will publish directives on behalf of the CSO defining the scope and sequence of staff actions.

I expect the Chiefs of these offices and Director of Staff to make service-level decisions aligned with this guidance and keep me informed through candid, timely communication.

FIELD COMMANDS

Like our forward-looking headquarters structure, our field command structure flattens our force structure from five echelons to three and reflects a mission-focused force design.

The Space Operations Command (SpOC) will be the primary force provider of space forces. The SpOC generates ready space forces for presentation to the Joint Force via the Commander of Space Forces (COMSPACEFOR).

The Space Systems Command (SSC) is responsible for developing, acquiring, and fielding effective and resilient space capabilities. SSC will be responsible for developmental testing, launch, on-orbit checkout, sustainment, and maintenance of USSF space systems, as well as integration with other space development activities including coordinated capability development with multi-national partners. In addition, SSC will provide oversight and integration of USSF science and technology initiatives. SSC will lead efforts to adapt our acquisition culture, workforce, and practice to match the pace of partners who are significantly accelerating space technology development.

Space Training and Readiness Command (STARCOM) will educate and train space professionals and conduct operational test and evaluation of systems in order to deliver combat-ready space forces prepared to succeed in our warfighting domain. While currently provisionally organized as a Delta, it will grow to a full-strength field command in fiscal year 2021. Our very near-term doctrine development, training, and education paradigms depend heavily on Air Education and Training Command and Air University. STARCOM, in coordination with the HCO, will develop options to establish a more independent system of doctrine and professional military education by 2023.

DISTRIBUTED DECISION AUTHORITY, "COMMAND BY NEGATION," AND MISSION COMMAND

Agile decision-making capability must extend outside headquarters and staff structures as well. Commanders, directors, and supervisors at the lowest competent and authorized level should be empowered to make decisions. Clear communication of delegated authorities is critical to empower effective and timely decision making. I expect headquarters elements to publish, and commanders to understand such authorities.

The potential speed and scale of space warfare means a traditional "command by affirmation" style, where a subordinate echelon assumes they are limited to narrowly prescribed authorities unless explicitly authorized by higher echelons, likely incurs a dangerous disadvantage. Therefore, I direct a default command style of "command by negation" where subordinate echelons are expected to default to action except where a higher echelon has specifically reserved authority.

In order to capitalize on unique opportunities of our small mission-focused Service, and to enhance conditions for initiative at all levels, **I am directing use of mission command by the Space Force.** Joint Publication 3-0 describes mission command as "built on leaders at all echelons who exercise disciplined initiative and act aggressively and independently to accomplish the mission," and that aligns with the bold, agile, innovative force we are developing. We will use "mission-type orders" (MTO) to direct subordinate echelon action, and work with USSPACECOM to implement MTOs to enhance resilient and responsive command and control of operational space forces.

Soon, Commanders at all levels must be prepared to engage in combat operations enhanced by artificial intelligence to observe, orient, decide and act at machine speeds. Anticipating the incorporation of automation into our decision making and C2 structures, STARCOM will prepare Commanders with the skill to develop and publish MTOs that are both human and machine executable. We will train our space professionals and the intelligent systems that support them to make deliberate, conditions-based delegations of authority or transitions between human-on-the-loop, human-in-the-loop, or autonomous modes of operation, consistent with appropriate human judgement, to maintain decision advantage under contested conditions.

Develop Joint Warfighters in World Class Teams

A NEW KIND OF JOINT WARFIGHTER

Every Service presents warfighters with a common sense of duty to Nation and devotion to mission. Every Service also presents warfighters with characteristics that reflect their unique domain. **We are America's space warfighters.** We share expertise and technical fluency with other space-oriented organizations, but space professionals are charged with mastering both space domain knowledge and unique operational art to achieve military purposes. **The character of war in the space domain is fundamentally unique from warfare in other domains.** This necessitates unique systems, tactics, and doctrine, and a dedicated cadre of warfighting professionals with specialized education, training, and experience to prevail in combat.

A VALUES-DRIVEN SERVICE

Core values are our Polaris. Our success depends on a solid foundation of shared personal values to enable agility, innovation, empowerment, mission command, and partnership. We expect all members to understand, exemplify and reinforce our core values.

Until we develop and finalize thoughts on core values with insights from Space Force leaders at all levels, we will keep as our foundation the Air Force core values – "integrity first, service before self, and excellence in all we do."

DIVERSITY & INCLUSION

Our Space Force is charged with protecting the people and ideals of the United States. Inclusion of professionals with diverse backgrounds, skills, and experiences enhances our ability to achieve national security objectives by increasing our ability to re-frame complex problems and inoculate against groupthink and bias.

We have a unique opportunity for a fresh start to create new policies, from dress and appearance, to family needs, personal development, and facility standards that are more consistent with inclusion efforts. The Space Force will not sustain an industrial-era accession paradigm that placed a premium on conformity and de-emphasized members' unique culture and heritage.

We value members for the culture they bring _with them_ into the Service and believe people of all backgrounds who are inspired by our mission and committed to our standards make the Space Force stronger. We will not accept either conscious or unconscious bias in our midst and support policies that actively guard against discrimination.

INFORMATION AGE RECRUITING AND RETENTION

Future growth projections and missions require additional space professionals and we want the best and brightest. In order to meet the demand, the HCO will lead efforts to develop recruiting partnerships at institutions that are recognized pipelines for technical talent from diverse backgrounds. The HCO will also develop a robust marketing campaign that encompasses experiential, partnership, media, and literature marketing to increase overall public and pre-accession interest in space. We will not passively wait for the best to respond to marketing, but actively use merit and diversity-based criteria to seek the talent we want.

Our efforts to manage, develop, and retain this talent will be central to the long-term viability and success of the Service. Our small, flat organization allows for deliberate individualized development focused on building space warfighters with the necessary experience and skills to prevail in combat while giving them the opportunities and benefits they seek for a fulfilling career. The HCO will maximize the full range of existing civilian and military personnel authorities, including those contained in recent changes to Law such as Modified Direct Hire Authorities.

We will monitor competition for talent from other DoD and civilian organizations looking to hire USSF space professionals. We will provide developmental opportunities for space professionals across all U.S. space sectors, including national security, civil, and commercial. We will recruit professionals with recognized expertise and unique experience able to perform immediately, as well as to build a junior cadre with the potential to grow into future leaders and innovators. We will create opportunities to crossflow high caliber personnel from industry into government positions and USSF members to industry or other government agencies to remain current in technology and best practices.

REALISTIC TRAINING

We will make every effort to train in realistic, contested conditions. Our forces are always in competition, and our capabilities are likely among the first targets of an aggressor's action. In both competition and conflict adversaries will seek to impose fog and friction through degraded systems, compromised networks, false information, and disrupted communication. We will develop and acquire in hi-fidelity simulators, virtual and augmented reality, and artificial intelligence to improve warfighting proficiency against a thinking, reacting adversary and foster the critical thinking and decision-making skills required in combat.

Commanders at all levels must ensure crew commanders and Mission Directors are proficient at applying warfighting concepts like acceptable level of risk, self-defense, risk to mission, and risk to force, and prepared to make sound tactical decisions in a contingency. We will recognize and reward expert system management and prudent risk acceptance to meet commander's intent.

CRITICAL THINKING AND COMMUNICATION

A lean, agile, and mission-focused force requires a high degree of connection, collaboration, and communication at all levels. We value a culture that actively shares insights and information, and provides context up and down echelons of command to ensure our space professionals understand their mission, commander's intent, and updates that align evolving requirements. We value clear verbal and written communication oriented to inform decisions and implement actions.

We also value design approaches to critical thinking, and data-driven problem solving. Over the next year, the Director of Staff will publish guidance that establishes a standard for how space professionals approach structured data-driven decision-making. Like MTOs, a standardized process is not intended to constrain thinking but rather to enhance our ability to rapidly analyze complex problems, develop and evaluate courses of action, and select a best option.

PROFESSIONAL EDUCATION

As the lead military Service for space, we will foster the synchronization and integration of space warfighting doctrine across our sister Services and National, Joint, and Combined operations. We will prioritize training and education courses for space professionals and optimize coursework to keep pace with advancing space employment demands. Space professionals will also gain experience from advanced education, selected space duty assignments, and broadening tours in Joint and Coalition environments.

In order to build tactical depth and operational leadership in our space professionals, we will focus leader development on specialization in our seven spacepower disciplines. We will build experts in these disciplines through advanced training and education that expands upon the space warfighting fundamentals taught at Undergraduate Space Training. STARCOM will develop the unique curricula required by the first four disciplines of Orbital Warfare, Space Electromagnetic Warfare, Space Battle Management, and Space Access and Sustainment. In addition, STARCOM will facilitate inclusion of space-unique content for Military Intelligence, Cyber Operations, and Engineering and Acquisition career fields for individuals intending to join or support Space Force units.

Beyond formal education, every space professional is expected to improve themselves and their teammates to better contribute to their teams. Leaders at all levels have a responsibility to enable and encourage the growth of their subordinates. We embrace a growth mindset and lifelong learning, allowing us to evolve and adapt to changing environments faster than our adversaries.

COMMITMENT TO FAMILIES

Our ability to retain diverse, talented and highly skilled space professionals is directly linked to our ability to meet the needs and expectations of their families. Just as we support the development and growth of Space Force members, we support the development and growth of Space Force families. We will work with our partners in the Air Force to improve access to childcare, housing, employment opportunities, and resources that make service in the Space Force attractive. We will develop and employ human capital management tools to reduce the tension between a member's military career and professional opportunities for their family members.

Deliver New Capabilities at Operationally Relevant Speeds

ANALYTICAL INSIGHTS DRIVING FORCE DESIGN

Service-level wargames over the past few years have focused on peer adversary conflict scenarios. Insights from these wargames inform future force development and highlight the potential for space warfighting capabilities to dramatically enhance the effectiveness, efficiency, and flexibility of our Joint Force.

Wargames have shown in any great power conflict, our alliances and partnerships are an essential factor to achieve success. **We will enable and defend our allies as they in turn provide capabilities that complement our own.**

The absence of features equivalent to national borders in space means there is no sovereign territory separating forces. While separation of terrestrial forces creates opportunity for early warning, defense by maneuver, and deterrence by credible escalation capabilities, the current lack of equivalent norms in space allows actors to operate at any location in the domain and at any distance from other spacecraft. This may allow a potential attacker to maneuver close to other space assets, from where they can execute a "first mover" surprise attack. This creates a potentially destabilizing "use it or lose it" dilemma that accelerates escalation. To avoid this dilemma, our force design must reduce vulnerability to a first mover attack and provide calibrated escalation options for Joint Commanders to seize or regain initiative.

Further, wargaming shows that space forces have inherent vulnerabilities in multiple domains. Space operations depend on orbital, terrestrial, and link segments. Each of these offers an attack surface, and adversaries will target vulnerable segments to degrade the larger architecture. We must ensure Joint Commanders are prepared to defend critical space assets that enable Joint Forces.

PROGRAMMATIC DIRECTION

The ability to prevail in conflict is foundational to all other Space Force missions. While America's legacy military space capabilities have been in the fight enabling combat effects for decades, our systems have not been consistently designed for war that initiates in, or extends to, the space domain. Adapting legacy designs will not produce effective systems for conflict because combat considerations favor fundamentally different design and engineering choices.

Our programs of record will deliver *Joint Warfighting* capabilities, providing Combatant Commanders military capability to achieve operational objectives. We will enable Combatant Commanders to protect and defend the people and homeland of the United States and our interests and allies. **I am willing to take risk in legacy system capacity and availability in order to create recapitalization opportunities for next-generation resilient and defensible systems.** Our force design must reflect data-driven, threat-informed choices that are stressed against the forecast capabilities of potential great power adversaries.

In order to establish a consistent structure for developing programmatic positions, I am establishing a Space Warfighting Analysis Center (SWAC) built on the foundation of the Enterprise Strategy and Architectures Office (ESAO) and the Space Security and Defense Program (SSDP). The SWAC will develop future force design options for consideration and CSO decision. SWAC analysis will support effective communication with Executive and Legislative resourcing and oversight functions.

To ensure our force design offers the Joint Force assured effects, the SWAC will analyze opportunities to enhance the resilience of legacy systems as an interim step to fielding a force designed to operate in a warfighting domain. The SWAC will develop future force structures that meet evolving mission requirements, are resilient to the threat, and are cost-informed. The SWAC will execute Service wargaming functions that help to formulate these architectures, as well as understand their interplay between USSF and the Joint Force. SWAC designs inform the CPG, annual "Force Design" updates, Service requirements, and programming options validated by the SRO.

Programmatic options will consider partner and hybrid architectures where appropriate, including with other U.S. government agencies. In the case of space-based environmental monitoring, some tactical satellite communications, and positioning, navigation and timing, civil and commercial partner services provide a degree of capability that may allow further re-investment in next-generation warfighting systems.

In the near term, the Space Force benefits from government and commercial partnerships to rapidly enhance capabilities in Space Launch and Sustainment and Space Domain Awareness. We will prioritize investments in Orbital Warfare, Space Electromagnetic Warfare, and tactical intelligence portfolios to enable effective defensive options and prompt offensive capability to deter adversaries from initiating conflict in or extending conflict into space. If deterrence fails, these capabilities posture us to fight and win in space.

OPERATIONALLY RELEVANT ACQUISITION SPEED

While our mission in space has evolved dramatically, shifting from strategic to operational and finally tactical warfighting, our acquisition paradigm has remained largely static. Current acquisition processes often require years from validating capability gaps to new fielded capabilities, even when the technologies involved are well known and program risks are low.

With DAF support, we will seek new acquisition authorities critical to enable the Space Force to streamline requirements validation; accelerate decision speed; maximize budget execution, stability, flexibility, and efficiency; increase program capability; and accelerate contracting speed. These changes will allow us to outpace adversaries unencumbered by industrial-era acquisition and oversight paradigms and consider new technology opportunities in which we can capitalize. This requires new delegated authorities in law or policy in some cases, and more effective utilization of existing authorities in others. We commit to providing the transparency required for effective oversight by Congress and other stakeholders.

ENHANCING COMPETITIVE ADVANTAGE

According to the 2017 National Security Strategy "adversaries and competitors [have become] adept at operating below the threshold of open military conflict and at the edges of international law." Adversaries actively create and exploit "gray zones" in which they achieve political objectives through actions that avoid traditional triggers for conflict where the United States enjoys clear military advantage. The Space Force will provide unique space-enabled options, tailored to support operational commanders, to shrink gray zones. Space Domain Awareness, for instance, enables attribution that reveals illegal or hostile action and sets conditions for a better informed and legitimized response.

Our design for force transformation must consider opportunities to enhance America's civil and commercial spacepower. Both Space Policy Directive-4 and statutory provisions of Title 10 task the USSF to protect America's interests, including commercial interests in space. The recent Space Force 2020 *Space Industrial Base Report* described a role the Space Force can play to help promising commercial partners thrive through high-risk initial ventures to validate high-potential new technologies. Space Force will use strategic investments to cultivate a strong, diverse and competitive American space industrial base. Civil and commercial developments that pave the way for exploration and commercialization beyond near-Earth orbit will both generate technology that benefits the USSF and require an order of magnitude expansion of our ability to sense, communicate and act to protect and defend American interests in cis-lunar space and beyond.

Expand Cooperation to Enhance Prosperity and Security

Evolved and expanding partnerships will improve our enterprise capability, capacity, and resilience. We will build on existing relationships and identify opportunities to integrate partner space capabilities into our enterprise.

JOINT INTEGRATION

Our closest partner will be the Air Force, on whom we will rely for enablers to accomplish tasks common to both of our missions. The Air Force will operate our bases, help us communicate throughout our global footprint, and deliver care and services for space professionals and their families.

We will undertake deliberate effort to enhance partnership with all Services by participating in both Joint and Service wargames and capability development efforts to understand their space equities, multi-domain concepts, enabling requirements and integration opportunities.

Space professionals must be expert integrators and communicators to ensure Joint counterparts in all Services and at all levels understand fast evolving space capabilities and threats, and their operational implications. To ensure Joint Force commanders are better equipped to utilize space domain-unique warfighting capabilities the COO will lead engagement to update space training modules in the JFMCC, JFLCC, JFACC, and JTF training courses to increase awareness of space warfighting capabilities as both independent and integrated operational options. In addition, over the next year STARCOM will work with the National Security Space Institute to develop updated space warfighting training modules in fulfillment of USSPACECOM joint training requirements.

In order to ensure service members from multi-Service backgrounds can better consume and contribute to USSF planning and direction, I am directing use of Joint planning methodology throughout the Space Force. In addition, we will template to Joint style, formats, and terminology unless explicitly required by DAF direction. This ensures a common standard and prepares USSF members for integration with Joint forces.

INTELLIGENCE COMMUNITY INTEGRATION

The need for space domain intelligence continues to increase in the face of changing missions and emerging threats. The U.S. Space Force will continue to strengthen its partnerships across the Intelligence Community, especially with the Defense Intelligence Agency, National Geospatial-Intelligence Agency, National Reconnaissance Office, and National Security Agency. Current cooperation is largely focused on the mission to protect and defend assets and must grow into operational collaboration at multiple levels. Today we are building deeper alignment across multiple agencies. In the future we will develop and expand shared strategies that synchronize national security space capabilities and operations to detect and characterize threats, defeat attacks, and respond to aggression.

As a focal point for space domain intelligence, we will seek to re-align space-oriented functions of the National Air and Space Intelligence Center to form a co-located National Space Intelligence Center (NSIC). In concert with the Space Force ISR Enterprise, the NSIC will provide a framework for growth to meet anticipated demand for increased space intelligence at foundational, tactical, operational and strategic levels.

MULTI-NATIONAL COOPERATION

Our efforts to deter and promote stability are enhanced by a multi-national effort. We will leverage ally and coalition partner capabilities in operations and acquisitions to identify and close gaps in our space enterprise. **We will take measures to strengthen our allies' space capabilities.** This includes cooperative capability development, professional education and training, and operational coordination and liaison. As we expand our network of partners, we will strive to be the partner of choice, providing the collective security for all those who join alongside us.

When space was a less contested domain, America could prefer security at the expense of collaboration. The evolution of the security environment requires greater interoperability with partners and allies, many of whom have already integrated with U.S. combat capability in other domains. We will reevaluate data sharing agreements and security paradigms that often limit coalition interoperability in space. We will expand partner participation in operations and capability development in order to reduce cost, increase resilience, and accelerate capability modernization.

Our approach to partnering also includes U.S. industry, civil organizations, academia, laboratories, and agencies. Key enablers for this effort are the scalable architectures and open standards which will also allow rapid, cost-effective integration of all desired partners.

Create a Digital Service to Accelerate Innovation

ESTABLISHING A DIGITAL SERVICE

Data and information, along with the skills and tools to put them to use, and drive to innovate will guide and accelerate our decision-making and permeate all the key activities of the Space Force.

Harnessing the best that technology has to offer and applying it in ways that can outpace the advances of our adversaries require us to change our capability development processes. **We will lead efforts to implement *Digital Engineering* standards for Space Force acquisition programs.** This will include adopting digital twins and model-based systems engineering, and expanding agile software development and DevSecOps to expedite capability development and improve acquisition outcomes. America's most successful companies, including hardware manufacturers, logistics providers, software companies, and "big data" analytics producers, employ these techniques to create competitive advantage for their businesses. These activities are also required of America's Space Force, and we will take industry's best practices, tools and benchmarks to create similar agility in military space development and operations.

Effectively harnessing technology requires the Space Force to foster and grow a *Digital Workforce*. Our personnel must be comfortable with technology and have ability to apply and adapt it for our national security

objectives. They should be capable of thinking and acting in the "data space," prioritizing data-centric solutions over product-centric processes. In addition, we will develop organic modeling acumen among USSF members to guide our digital efforts. This will make us more capable and engaged partners with industry and allow us to implement a more digital acquisition paradigm using modeling and simulation. Digital fluency will begin with state-of-the-art training environments and is sustained through continued exposure and implementation of digitally supported decision-making throughout their careers.

With digital engineering and fluency as foundational elements, we will drive *Digital Operations* across our space mission sets to increase all domain awareness and close the kill chain faster with more robust, informed C2 decision options. In doing so, we will fully exploit modern commercially-based digital capabilities including software defined networks, data analytics, machine intelligence, cloud edge computing, and modular plug-n-play systems. Digital applies not only to our weapon systems but to our business processes as well, and the Space Force will apply similar techniques to enable a Digital Headquarters. Full implementation of our digital strategy will involve investments in Digital Engineering data and analytics infrastructure to ensure all our data is discoverable, accessible, understandable, linked, and trusted across multiple security levels.

Automation and autonomy will accelerate and streamline our operations and provide analytics to optimize mission and headquarters effectiveness. Applying machine learning and trusted levels of autonomy will allow our personnel to focus on data-driven decision-making instead of manually sorting and sense-making the vast amounts of data created by operations in space.

Our investments in this digital campaign will be effective if they allow us to make better use of our human capital. By automating tasks that are repetitive, time-consuming, or that do not require application of human intelligence, we will create the time to train, educate, wargame, and develop a world-class fighting force. This will also give us an advantage in recruiting and retaining space professionals who expect to work with cutting edge cognitive tools. The TIO will lead automation and digitization efforts over the next year to generate a 15% enhancement in the amount of dwell time available for advanced training.

⚵ *Summary*

Space is a vital national interest. Activities on land, at sea, in the air, through cyberspace, and in the electromagnetic spectrum all depend on space superiority. The nation established the U.S. Space Force to ensure freedom of action for the United States in, from, and to space. The strategic environment demands we act boldly now to build a Service designed to act with speed and decisiveness to ensure the United States maintains its advantage in the domain.

By executing this guidance, we will support a position of strategic stability, U.S. advantage in space, and a space warfighting posture that deters aggression and ensures Joint and Coalition warfighters can employ forces in the time, place, manner, and domain of our choosing.

While not all encompassing, this CPG is sufficient to provide clear guidance on the way forward. I expect all uniformed and civilian space professionals, and USAF personnel assigned to USSF units and staffs, to read and begin implementing this guidance immediately. Soon, the USSF Director of Staff will publish an implementation plan to accompany this guidance that offers specified and implied tasks derived from the CPG, the offices of primary responsibility, and timelines.

This CPG identifies those characteristics and capabilities within the force that must evolve. We do not have the luxury of delay for further analysis. We will move out to build the Service our nation expects and needs. I am excited to join you in this journey.

JOHN W. RAYMOND
General, USSF
Chief of Space Operations

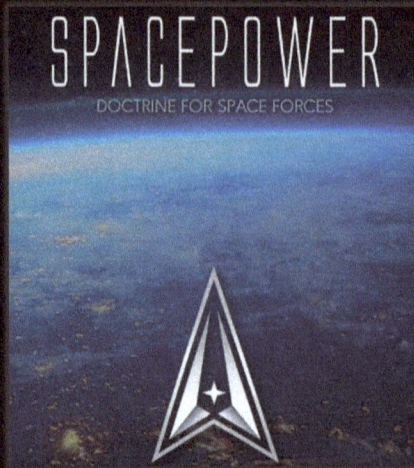

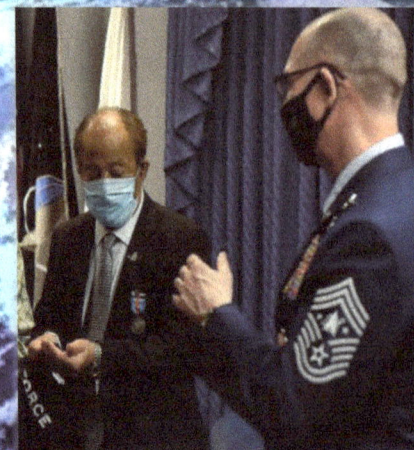

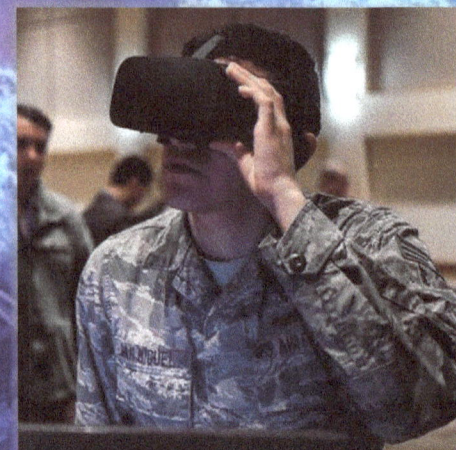

www.ingramcontent.com/pod-product-compliance
Lightning Source LLC
Chambersburg PA
CBHW080646110426
42813CB00009B/2603